I0488174

The Ultimate Tattoo Course

The Complete Tattoo Apprentice Guide

By Scott Wolfe

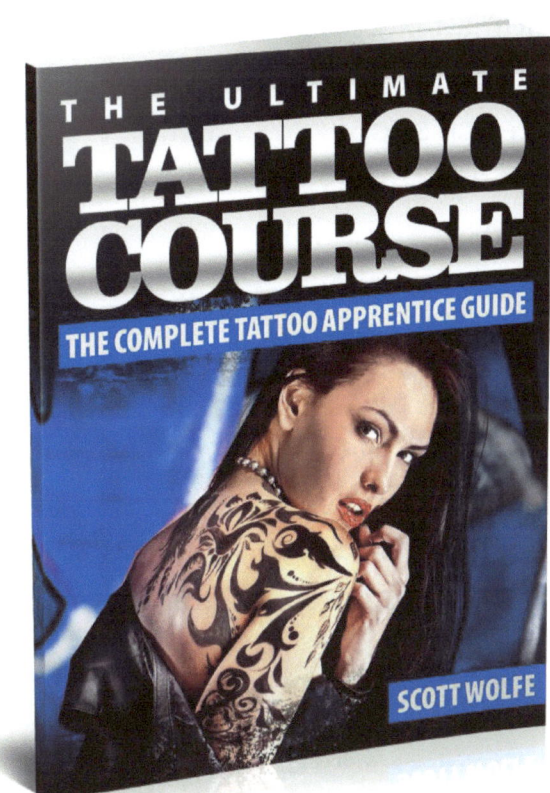

The Ultimate Tattoo Course

The Complete Tattoo Apprentice Guide

Copyright 1999-2014 by The Ultimate Tattoo Course. All Rights Reserved.

Chapter 1- Introduction

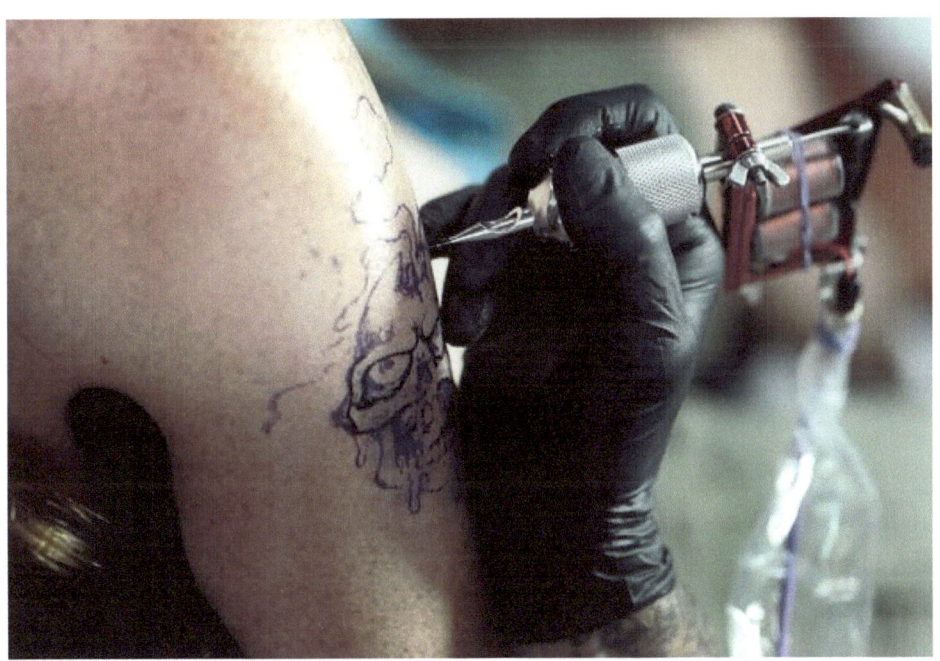

Hi, I'm Scott Wolfe I'm a former tattoo artist originally from small town USA now residing in California. I have tattooed for 15 years and have worked all over the world and have had the experience of being able to work with some of the best artists in the world and work in some of the coolest shops. I now spend my time painting and spending time with my family and working on cars. I am not a writer; I just have had a lot of experience in tattooing and decided to write this book to help fellow artists get started in the field of tattooing.

Chapter 2- You're tattoo equipment

First thing to discuss is your tattoo equipment, this will be a long chapter because there is a lot of equipment to talk about. One of the most important things to first discuss is tattoo machines; your tattoo machine will make the difference between the quality of the work produced, low quality tattoo machines will produce low quality work obviously.

Low-quality machines will produce depressing lines, and spotty shade work. And it will even effect the healing times in the tattoo. Spending the money on the best machines is one of the most important things you can do to start off. Good quality tattoo machines can run you anywhere from $200 to 300 up to $600.

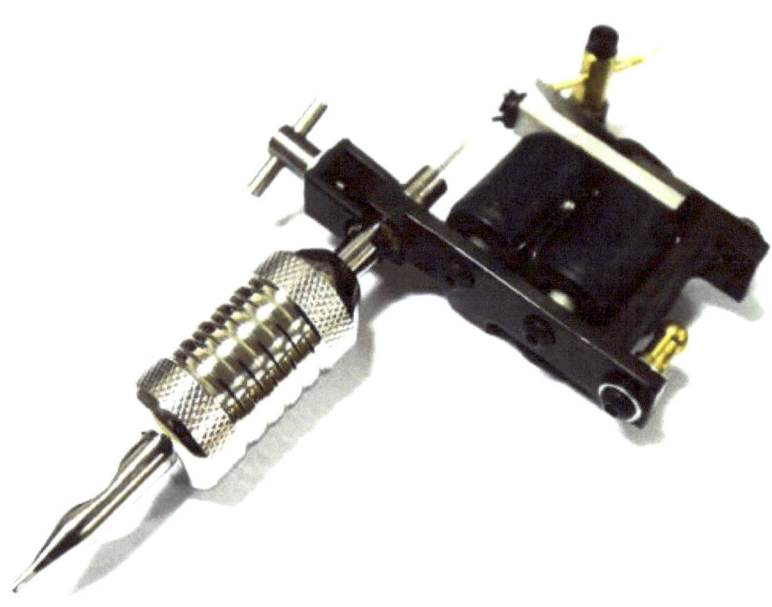

The Ultimate Tattoo Course

When you first start out it's hard to afford good machines. But even if you have to start with inexpensive machines just make sure there well-tuned. And try to upgrade as soon as you can. Many artists build up a huge assortment of tattoo machines over the years; you never know what occasion any given machine will call for. A wide assortment of power shaders, soft liners, and soft shaders should all be in inventory.

Then when I started tattooing years ago I started off with a set of next-generation G2 machines I think I got a set for around $300 for a liner and shader those machines lasted me many years, next-generation machines are known to be powerful and put in solid color. Once again there a little bit more expensive but it's worth it in the long run. Those machines lasted me at least five years before I sold them off, other good machines are Workhouse Irons, these are very durable tattoo machines. The tip is if you want to start off and get a good machine but not spend a lot of money is to maybe check on eBay, or Craigslist, you can get used machines which are not too bad because they're usually well broken in, this way you get started for cheap and still get high quality machines.

Tattoo equipment diagram:

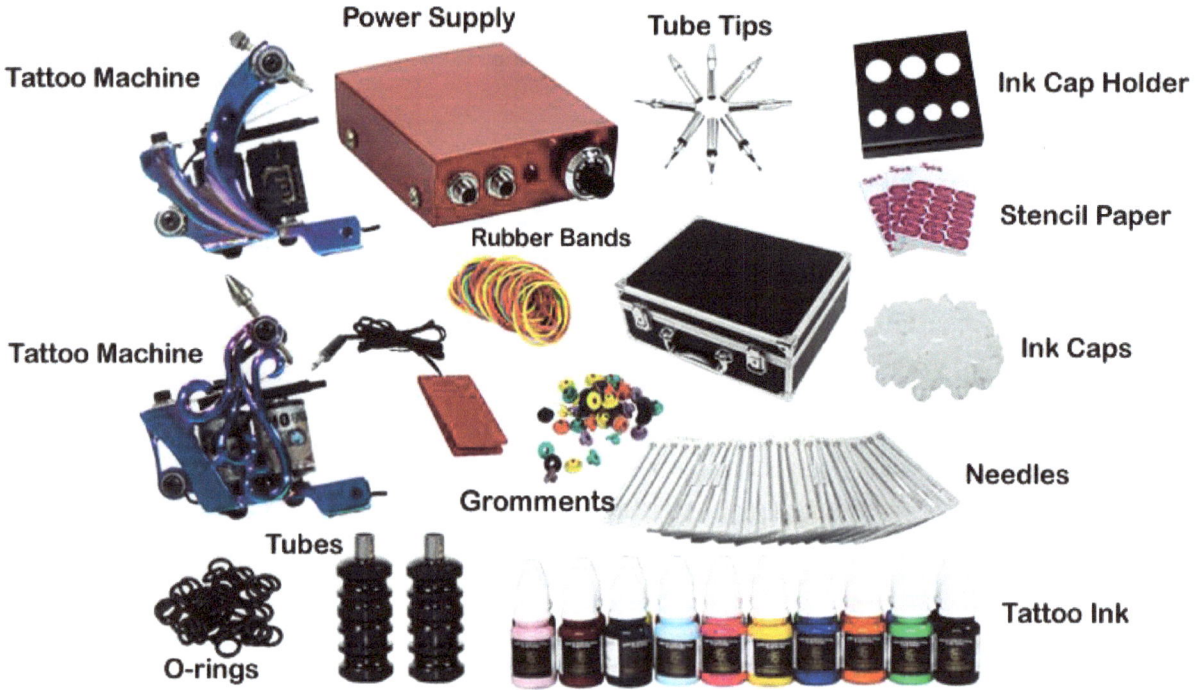

 Something else worth mentioning is some of the new rotary machines that have hit the market. Rotary machines have grown in popularity over the years many of the big names like Nikko Hurtado, Roman and a few others use Rotary machines. I myself have used rotary machines and traditional machines for about the last five years, there really good and you can even do line work with rotary machines. Most of all there known for their smooth shading and the smooth color work that you can do with them, definitely worth checking out.

Another thing you need is a good high quality power supply once, again if you go cheap. Honestly you stand the chance of the power supply cutting out on you, not being very powerful or just not lasting a long time. You can get a good cheap power supplies online for around $50, but it's best to spend the money, In the neighborhood from $100-$200 on high-quality digital power supply. once again you get what you pay for, I have a Demographics power supply that I bought back in 2000 and I literally still have that same power supply to this day in 2014 that power supply was $160, by far the best investment I've ever made.

The third thing I consider most important are your tattoo inks, there are many reputable companies available. Starbright, Eternal, MOMS Millennium, Dermaglo, all are very good quality inks and will cost you about $100-$200 for 7-12 1oz bottles. Tattoo Ink is not cheap for the good stuff. Once again it's best to get the best quality you can afford if you want nice bright color work and if you want the tattoo to last for a long time you're going to need quality tattoo ink.

Some other mentionables as far as your tattoo equipment are, needles we which we will discuss later, O-rings, rubber bands, gloves ,covers for your tattoo machine, your power supply, rubber grommets for your tattoo machine and various other things check the diagram to see more.

Chapter 3- Needles

As far as tattoo needles, tattoo needles might not seem very important but they are, good quality needles will produce better work and also help in healing times for the tattoo. Another thing that is important to have along with your tattoo needles is an eye loupe. And eye loupe is very important to have so you can check your needles in the middle of a tattoo; the last thing you want is a bent needle. A bent needle can hurt your customer and not only is it painful but it will ruin your tattoo and the last thing you want is to ruin a tattoo! That's loss of sales, potentially loss of customer. And you just don't want that news going around that you're hacking up tattoos.

There are many good companies to get tattoo needles definitely look around you can also make your own but it's a lot of work and you're going to need additional equipment to make your own needles. A needle jig and loose needles just to name a few of the things you will need. Consider a few extra hundred invested in that if you want to make your own. What's popular now is artists just buy a box of 50 pre sterilized needles, blister pack and already sterilized and that way once you're done you can just dispose of those needles and continue.

Chapter 4- Shop furniture

Shop furniture, you're going to need a few things to have a nice comfortable set up for your tattoo shop. For yourself you're going to want a nice comfortable chair, you're going to be sitting for hours on end sometime so you want a comfortable chair for those long periods.

Also a comfortable chair for your customer once again when you're sitting for hours on end to get a tattoo, you want everybody to be comfortable. You also want a nice clean workstation. Could be a desktop or counter, another thing artists use and I have used are the Craftsmen's work boxes. You can get these from Home Depot for around $100 each and they're really nice because you can store all of your equipment and you can also lock it away at night. It comes with a nice metal structure and metal top which makes it easily to clean if need be and once again you're able to securely store away all of your equipment and machines and lock the box.

After all you're hard work the last thing you want is to spend your money on high-quality machines and needles and then have them stolen. And you have to be careful with this. Many people and even other artists will pick up things for others stations. An armrest is also very important to do arm tattoos as well is having a massage table for bigger tattoos where you need the customer to lie down it's good for everybody as you can better access the area that you need to tattoo and your customer can lay down and relax while having the tattoo done.

Shop lighting:

Good shop lighting is worth having in your tattoo area and additional spotlights for hard to see areas, you don't want to try to tattoo in the dark it's very important to see all the shades and colors in the tattoo that you're applying. Shop lighting is very important. I can't stress it enough to have a nice clean and comfortable work area. I've done my best work in nice comfortable environment. Then you can just focus on the art and not other things, this is very important.

Chapter 5- Sterilization

The medical portion of your tattoo equipment also includes a lot of things. Here I will go through some of what is needed and its uses. First and foremost the most important thing needed is a tattoo autoclave. The tattoo autoclave is one of the most important pieces of the tattoo equipment because of what it does, the **tattoo autoclave** is what sterilizes all of your equipment which makes it safe for customers and yourself.

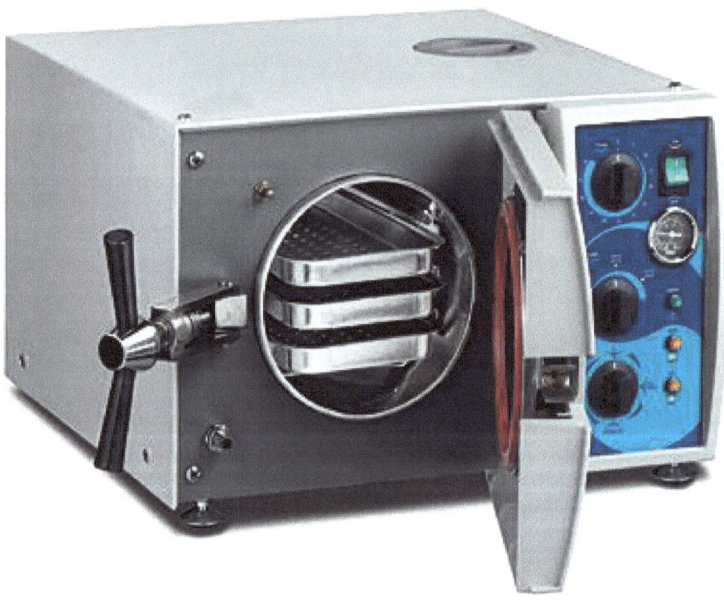

The **tattoo autoclave** is also going to be one of the more expensive items that you purchase for tattooing. Tattoo autoclaves can run anywhere from $500-$4000. Second is an ultrasonic this is needed to pre-breakup tattoo ink on your equipment before it goes into the autoclave it gets loosened. This is needed to also clean tattoo grips and piercing equipment before going into the autoclave.

An ultrasonic cleaner can run anywhere from $50 for a cheap one, up into $200 to $400 for really nice ones they are worth their weight in gold. Some of the other things you will need that covers the medical portion are gloves, many artists use Dettol, it can be used like Green soap for stencil removal and inside the tattoo process. Sterilization pouches and random sizes to fit your tattoo equipment and piercing equipment catching gloves and the equipment.

Chapter 6- Medical equipment

There's also a wide range of medical cleaning solutions that you'll use for cleaning your tattoo equipment and area all of these will be listed in the tattoo equipment:

Autoclave- tattoo equipment sterilization

Ultrasonic- jewelry device used to break up particles on your tattoo equipment before final cleaning and sterilization.

Alconox- for use with your ultrasonic, ultrasonic cleaner

Gloves- for tattooing and cleaning.

Dettol- like green soap. Used in the tattoo process for ink cleanup

Green soap- medical soap most commonly used in tattooing, has a great (distinctive tattoo shop smell)

Chapter 7- Art and stencil supplies

Next we talk about the stencil process and what's needed. Back in the day many artists used speed stick to apply stencils, while this works for some it's an outdated method. Now there's a new product called Stencil Stuff, there's also a wide assortment of other new products available but Stencil Stuff seems to be the most popular right now and it works well.

You will also use thermal paper to trace your stencil on before applying it to the skin; this thermal paper can cost about $30 for a box of 100s pieces. It's also important to have; it makes your job a million times easier. Alcohol pads are also used around this time, alcohol pads are used to clean the skin before applying the stencil. Then the stencil is traced on the thermal paper and applied to the skin, and then you want to let it dry for a few minutes before the tattoo procedure.

Chapter 8- Your tattoo machines

Once again tattoo machines are really important part of tattooing, without good quality machines you're not going to be tattooing the right way. Investing in machines will make or break your work. Many artists start off with cheaper tattoo machines and it's understandable at first, you can get a good entry-level tattoo machine from anywhere from $50-$150 but as soon as you start making money definitely upgrading to better machines is best. Good machines allow you to do better line work and smoother shading and accomplish deep bright colors.

Diagram of tattoo machine parts:

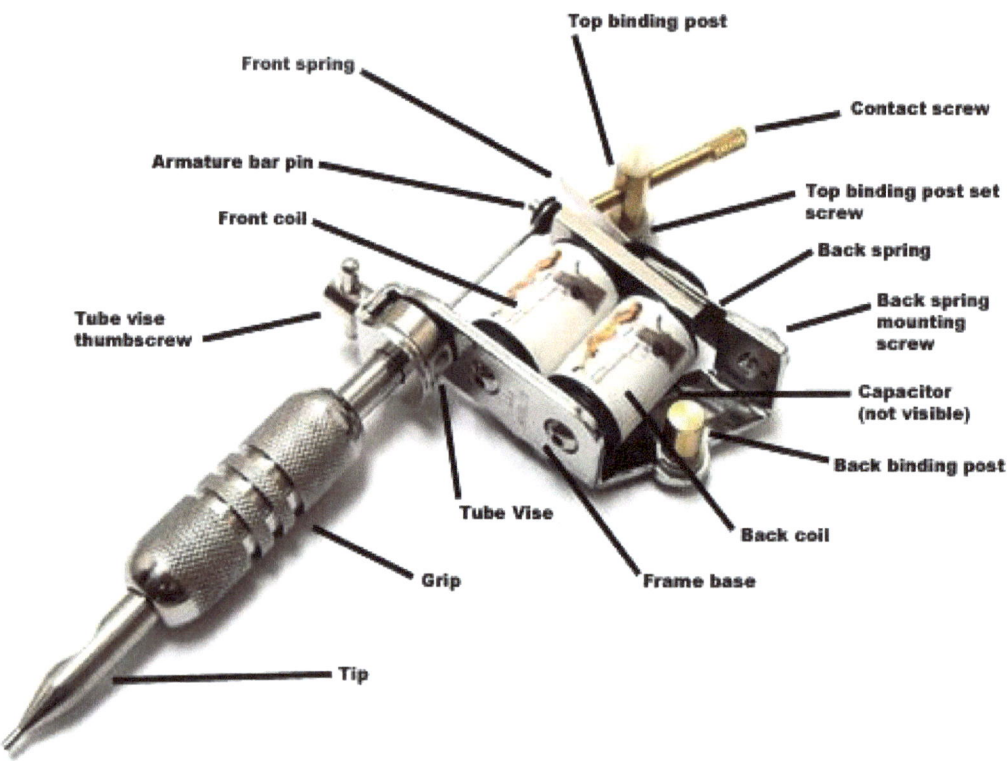

Many artists have a wide selection due to the wide ranges of lines and shading needed in tattooing. You will have some machines setup for power line-work. And well as some setup just for smooth shading.

Chapter 9- Machine tips

There are also now the new rotary style machines which are very popular for smooth shading and even better the healing times on rotary machines seem to be shorter. Artist usually have a wide selection of machines, don't feel bad if you are just starting out with one or two machines after the years you will accumulate tons more. It's not uncommon for an artist to have 10-20 or even more machines just lying around.

The thing is when start tattooing you will see each machine serves a different purpose and you'll accumulate machines based on your style of tattooing some days you're doing the bold traditional work which you will use a heavier heavier machine then one day you're doing just simple smooth black and gray and you may prefer to choose a rotary machine that day. That's why it's best to build up a nice supply of tattoo machines over the years I'll give you a list of tattoo machines and other quality companies that make quality tattoo machines at the end of this chapter.

Another thing is you want to make sure your machines are always in good operation, one thing that you definitely want to do is invest in a machine rebuild kit. Not only is it for rebuilding your machines but it also helps in maintaining your machines you'll find that after long sessions of tattooing and after a while of having the machine you have small parts to replace. Usually these parts are the coils or maybe the armature bar, o-rings, contact screw or the front and rear springs.

Also the capacitor can go out you can notice this pretty easily. You will see a bright spark from the contact screw and front spring when your capacitor is going out. The tattoo rebuild kit is also worth its weight in gold if you ever have any problems while tattooing and have to stop and break down your machine you definitely want to have all the right parts available to fix it.

Tattoo Machine Company list:

In no particular order.

1. Time Machine. Popular tattoo machines, very durable and long lasting. Great for all around general tattoos. These will never quit on you. These can run $250-$400 for a set.

2. Bishop Rotary (NEW Rotary machine) New Rotary machines built in California. Good company, great running machines.

3. Next Generation

4. Huck Spaulding. One of the oldest tattoo companies around. Very popular and trusted company.

5. Pulse

6. Dringenberg. Great machines, expensive, plan to spend $400-$600 for a machine atleast.

7. Aaron Cain

8. Iron Workhorse. A must for your tattoo arsenal. Very durable and powerful, always ready to put in hard work.

9. FK IRONS. Popular new company

10. Dragon Tattoo Supply- Starter tattoo machines from $40

Many of these are very high end machines and can range in price all the way up into the thousands for full setup for the machine and power supply needed to power it.

Tattoo Machine Parts.

A+D ointment- for prepping the skin, a thin coat before the tattoo is started.

O-rings- to hold the top springs.

Rubber bands- to hold the needle in place.

Tongue depressors- to spread the a&d and Vaseline.

Ink caps- to hold the ink.

Grommets- to hold the top on the needle on the armature bar.

Adjustment tools- various tools to tune your machine with.

Ink cap holder- to hold the ink caps in place.

Vaseline- to prep the skin to tattooing.

Saran wrap- to cover things in your work station and to cover the tattoo afterwards.

Chapter 10- Properly use needles

Your tattoo needles are also very important, you are to make sure you are careful un-packaging the needle and inserting it into the machine tube you want to make sure that you don't bend the needle, that will affect your customers comfort.

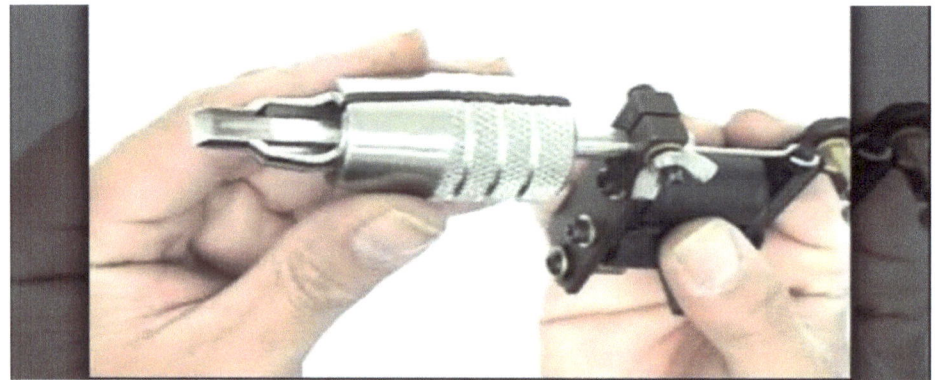

You also need to make sure you have a sharps container nearby for tattoo needle disposal; you're also going to need a spore testing company, this is an annual service that will do your autoclave spore testing. Also never ever reuse a tattoo needle for any reason. That is not the reputation you want to build.

Chapter 11- Practice skins

Practice skins come with a lot of tattoo kits that are available today. Another new item for tattoo practicing is called a "pound of flesh", also for sale online you can look it up I'm not very familiar with the product but I hear many good reviews about it. Not only can you use it for practice there's also a few other things you can use which is readily available. You can also use grapefruits, oranges and some people even use melons to practice on that will definitely help you practice your tattooing.

Chapter 12- Tattoo inks

This chapter is for tattoo ink and the various tattoo inks available. There are many great companies in the USA that produce great quality tattoo ink and not just the US but the UK produces some great inks like Derma-Glo which is now emerging on the scene. Derma-Glo can be a little hard to find in the USA just a few select dealers. Other inks worth mentioning are MOMS Millennium, Starbright and many others that I will list at the end of this chapter. Most quality tattoo inks will run anywhere from $70 up to $150-$200 for a set of 1 ounce bottles or half ounce bottles.

Tattoo Inks list in no particular order.

1. Starbright- Been around for ages. Battle tested and great all around ink.

2. Eternal- Another standard good quality ink

3. Kuro Sumi- Japanese Ink, The new color line is great. There mostly known for the black outlining ink, and there cherry shading ink, which gives a red effect to the tattoo

4. Intense- Tattoo Artist Mario Barths own ink. Worldwide known and trusted.

5. Millennium (MOMS) - Another good brand, been around for ages.

6. Dermaglo- My personal fave, the blues are awesome as well as the white and bright yellow.

7. Skincandy

Chapter 13- Sketching

What you want to have is a nice assortment of art tools for designing your tattoos. Many people these days like custom work and the tattoo industry is largely moving to custom designs to satisfy clients. Many people like unique artwork and request better work these days this is a good thing, but it will definitely keep you on your toes as far as keeping up with what's hot.

Many artists take time and can spend hours and hours working on a tattoo design for customer. You have to think, this will reflect on you so you want the best as possible for your clients. This is how you get your name out there as a great artist. Art supplies can include the sketchbook and maybe some tracing paper.

Drawing pencils and markers, **Prisma** colored pencils and **Prisma** color markers are extremely common and popular because of the bright colors that they give. Really vibrant beautiful work can be done with these **Prisma** color pencils and markers. Definitely worth checking out and will be added to your tattoo and art workstation. It's also common for artists to have a wide range of media including watercolors and even oil paint sometimes for your artwork in general.

Chapter 14- Making stencils

The process of making the stencil you'll need transfer paper to transfer the stencil to the skin. What's most commonly used is stencil stuff you can purchase stencil stuff online from Dragon Tattoo Supplies and its really good for applying stencils, most people years ago would use speed stick, it can also be used without a problem also. Making the stencil is relatively easy you basically make a copy with a copy machine of the tattoo design you want to use.

Basically put that over the piece of thermal paper and then trace out your stencil on that before applying it to skin with the stencil stuff or speed stick. Use a thin amount of either, or else you will make a mess and smudge the tattoo design. A thin coat is all that's needed. Then dab it with a paper towel, and allow it to dry for about 5-10 minutes if you really want it to stay.

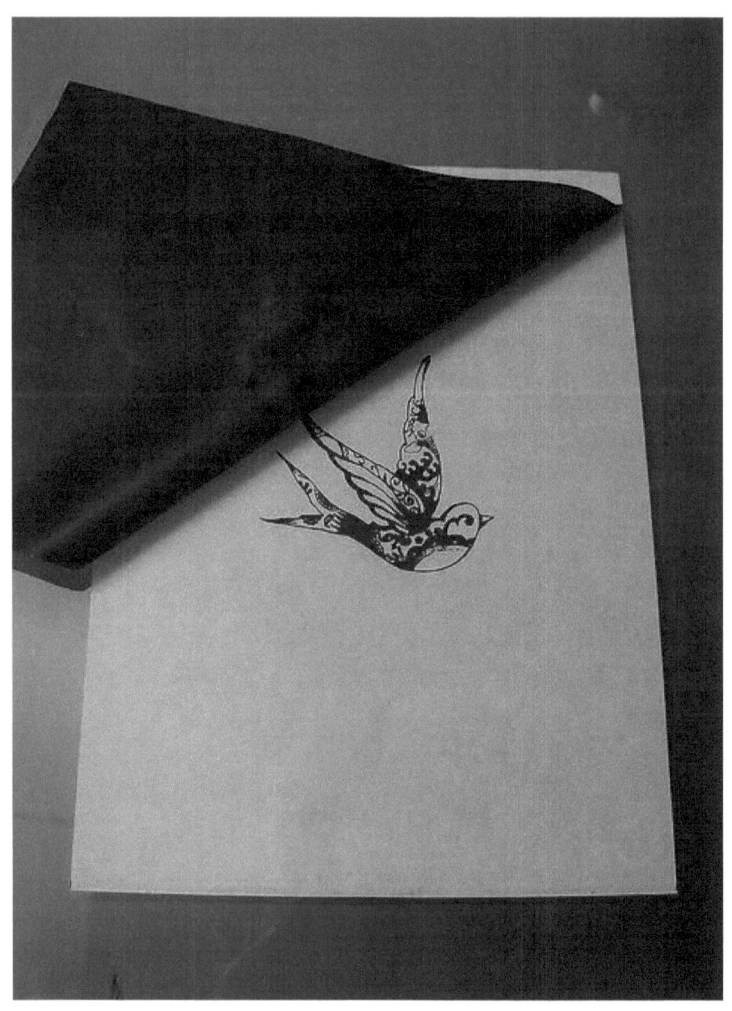

Chapter 15- Preparing machines and workstation

Your workstation should be a nice comfortable place that you can produce your tattoo art. You want to make sure you have comfortable chairs for you and your customer and have all of your equipment at arm's length or at least in close proximity. You don't want to have to get up or stop and do other things in the middle of your tattoo this can increase the chances for **cross contamination**. You want your tattoo area to be very orderly and neat.

The setup is a nice clean desktop and sometimes artists will use craftsman boxes, these come in handy because you can store all of your tattoo equipment and supplies away very easily and lock it up at night. And they're very easy to cleanup, sterilization is very important part of the tattoo procedure and in tattooing in general you want to make sure you have very clean and healthy practices always, not doing so puts you in jeopardy and your customer.

You want to make sure you have plastic for bottle covering, machine covering, and general covering of the area you're tattooing in. Also make sure you have proper lighting to be able to see when you cleaning up.

Chapter 16- Tattooing procedure

In the tattooing procedure you need a few things like alcohol pads to prep the skin, gloves on and paper towels to wipe the skin . Green soap for cleaning the tattoo while the procedures going on. A capful of green soap in a bottle filled with water is needed. You will also need a bottle of alcohol and a bottle for witch-hazel. I keep a separate bottle for each close by.

You want to make sure as you open the needles you are very cautious about being pricked you want to make sure that you don't poke yourself with the needle also make sure you have a sharps container for disposal of all of these things afterwards. You will need to dispose of the needle and the tubes whether their metal or plastic, plastic can be thrown away metal can be sent to the autoclave for sterilization after cleaning.

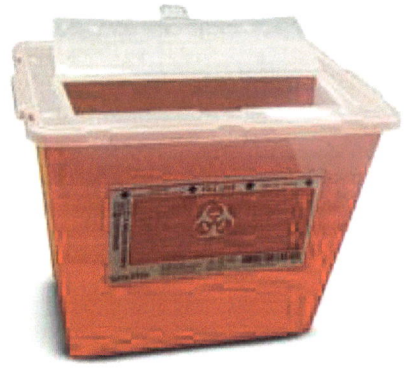

Chapter 17- Shading

Black and grey tattoos are extremely popular so you will have your fair share of shading to do.

There's a few things needed for shading I will discuss now.

Here's a list of things you will need:

1. Black tattoo ink of your choice. I prefer Talens black.
2. Several random size ink caps, I use large size
3. Witch hazel

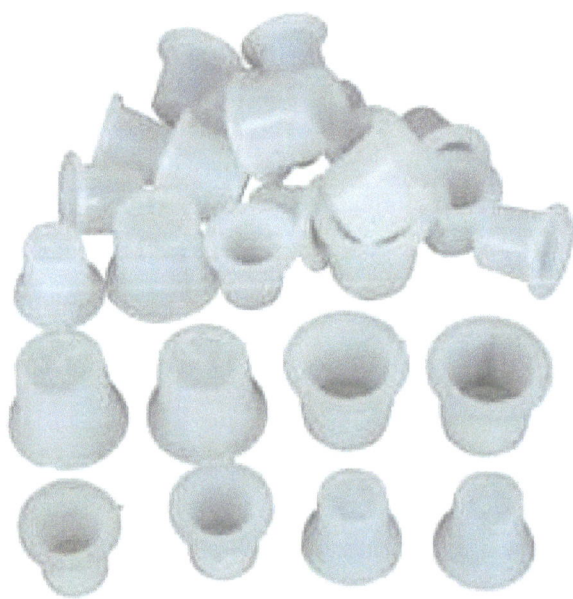

So this is the basic method that works for me to get the smoothest shading possible.

First I arrange my ink caps, usually 3-5 ink caps in a row.

Then for each ink cap I put drops of ink, in the first cap I put 1 drop of black ink in the next cap I put 3 drops of black ink, in the third cap I put 5-10 drops of black ink, in the 4th cap I fill it to 25% black ink and in the last cap fill it to the top with black ink

So it looks like this:

After the ink is in the caps I go back and **fill the rest of each cap with witchhazel**, water also works many people use distilled water, but I prefer witch hazel, seems to give me better consistency of smooth shade.

In the black and grey piece I usually start with the lighter shades and work those into the skin and dip into the darker shades as needed, I usually stick with the lightest shades only using the darkest if most needed, this gives you a lot of depth in your tattoo, also its best to work from light to dark as dark you cannot lighten. I have found this method to give me shading that I'm well known for. And it allows me to do work like this:

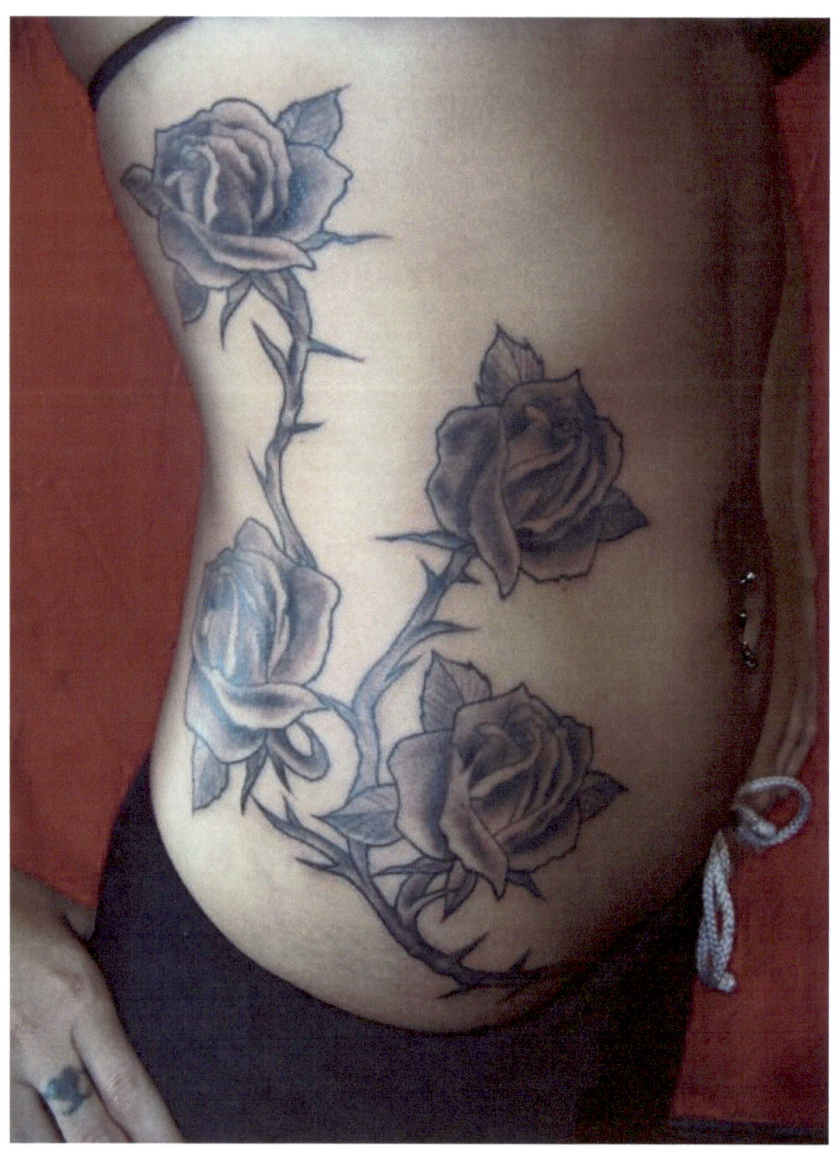

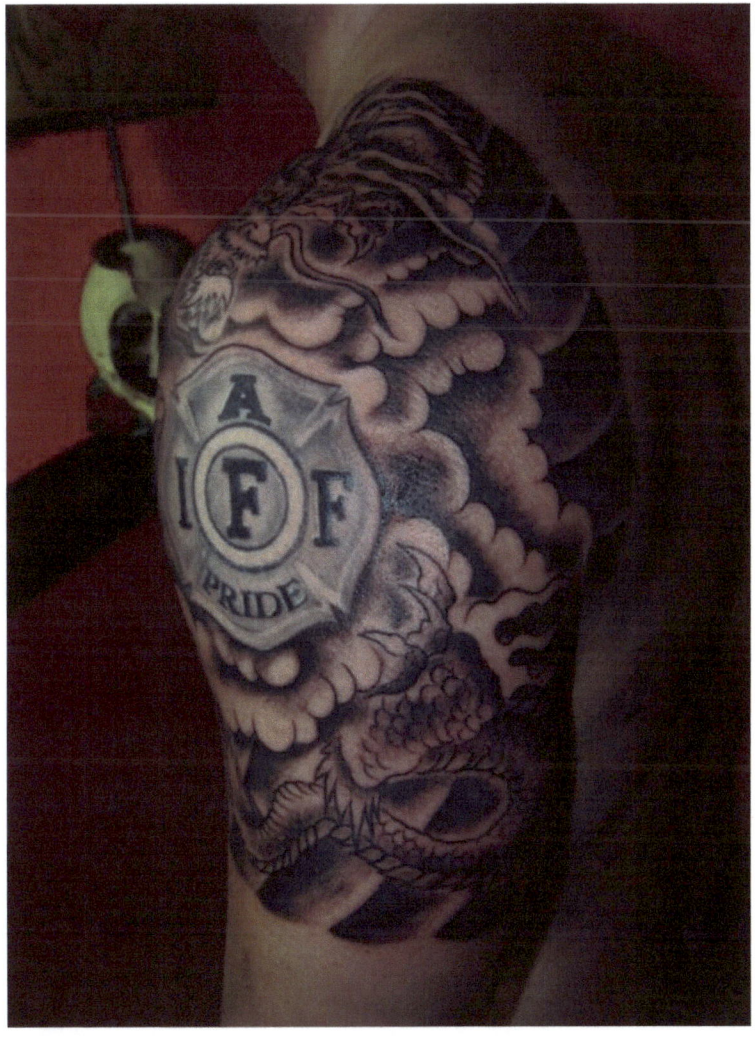

Coloring:

Same thing with black and grey as far as setup but there's a little difference on how to take on color pieces. For one you will want to make sure you have some A&D ointment close by and plenty ink caps for all your colors, between tattooing colors you have to make sure you prevent the mixing of colors, this can happen on the skin or in the ink cups, so you have to be very careful with this until you know what you are doing. Getting some black into white or yellow will dull the color fast and you won't get the brightest colors possible. Always have a cup full of water for washing out your machine tube between color changes, A little tip is I also spray a little green soap or whatever your using to clean the tattoo, I spray a little in the water to help with cleaning out the tube. It's a great little trick of mine.

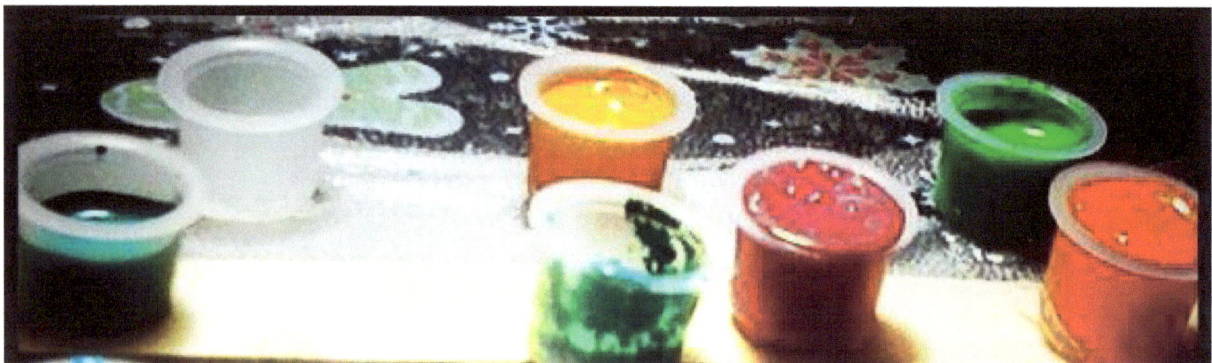

Make sure you angle the needles right when **working your color into the skin** a 45 degree angle is best to "work" the ink underneath the skin. Like in this picture:

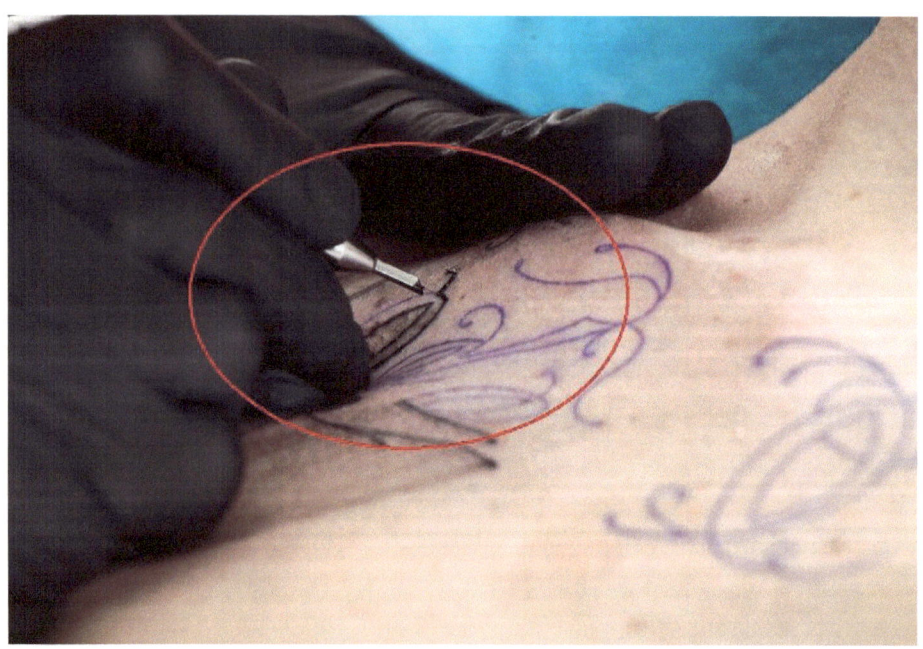

For bright colors here is a small list of companies I know of that produce very bright ink.

Dermaglo for their country blue, I love this color it's such a perfect color blue and can be used for everything requiring some blue.

Hot Pink by Kuro Sumi is a nuclear looking color pink, it's almost unreal that the color is that neon and looks the same on the skin. It's an amazing color to work with.

Starbright has a really amazing yellow. It's very bright and perfect for anything you need yellow for.

 I seldom water down or mix my ink like some do. But I also work at a relatively fast pace. And here is some of my color work:

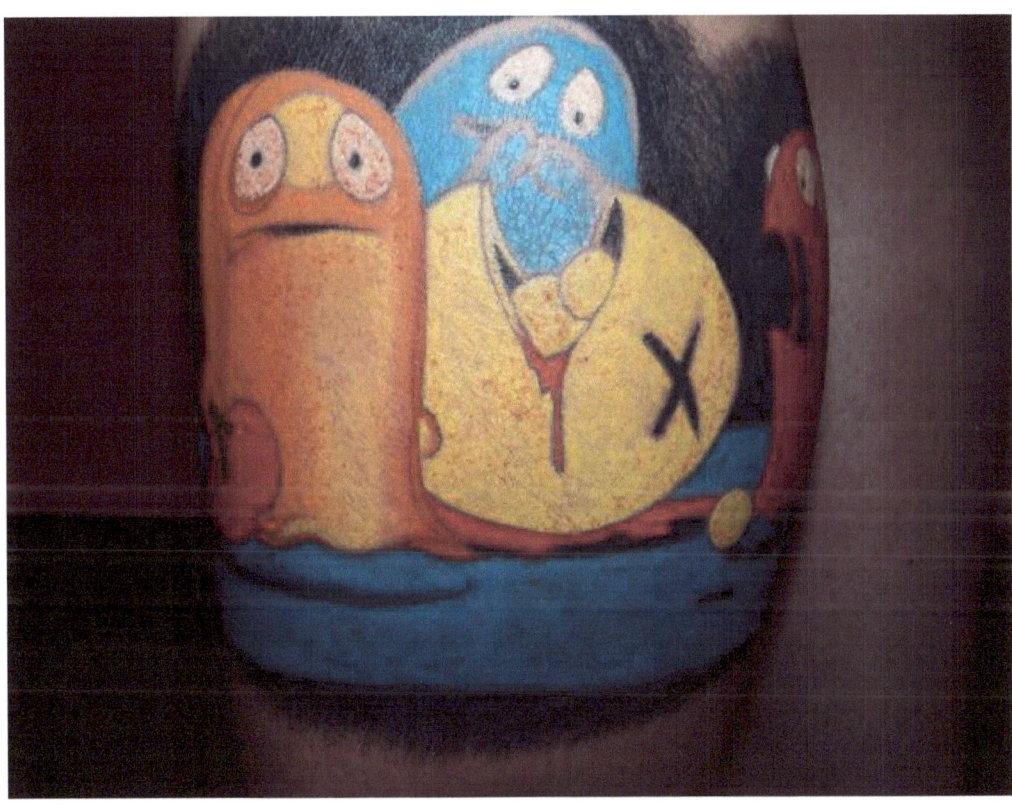

Chapter 18- Cleanup

Ok in this chapter we talk about cleanup and staying safe while tattooing. Keeping clean is very important in tattooing. A clean procedure and work station not only protects you but also your client. The last thing you want to be known for is giving someone a disease that will cancel your career right away.

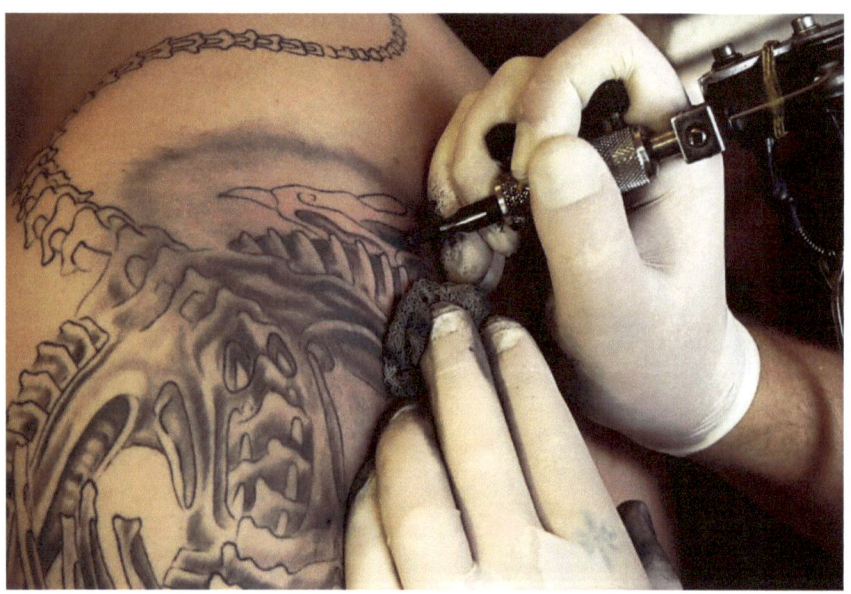

I'll list some tattoo cleaner and equipment needed for cleanup and sterilization.

Madacide- Disinfectant Cleaner, Broad spectrum multipurpose cleaner. **No Alcohol** content. **EPA registered.** Kills: **Influenza A.** HIV, HEPATITIS

A, B and C, TB, MRSA, VRE, and SARS. Fungicidal. More economical, lower unit cost. Safe to use. Non-toxic.

Green soap- Green Soap Tincture traditional Skin prep for both Tattoo and Piercing: Mix 10% Green Soap with 90% Distilled Water and clean the skin first.

Alcohol 50-90% preferred

Sterilization pouches

Autoclave

Ultrasonic cleaner.

Alconox

Tons of plastic wrap or barrier film

Gloves

Some people use aprons. To protect themselves and their clothes.

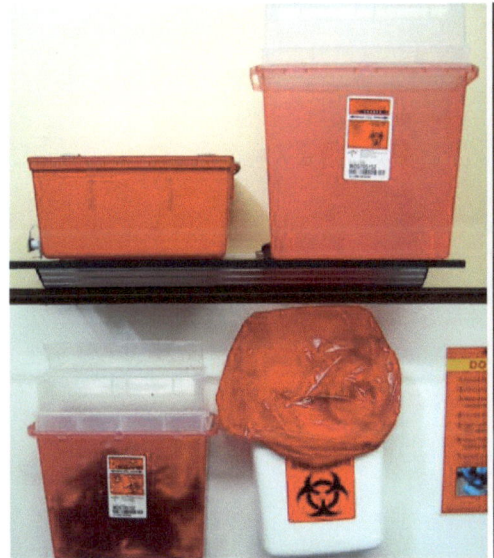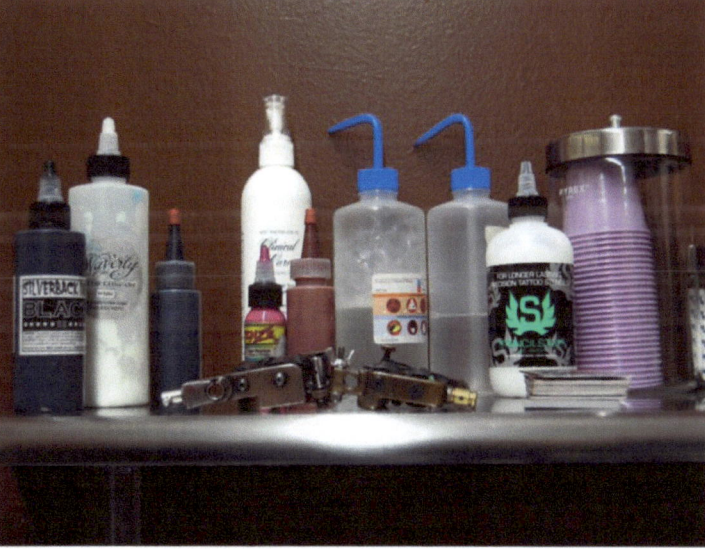

The Ultimate Tattoo Course

Chapter 19- Aftercare

Following the tattoo procedure come's aftercare. And healing color tattoos and black and grey are completely different. Colors tattoos are a little more sensitive, and need a little bit more help to heal perfectly. I recommend using A&D ointment to help color tattoos heal. With black and white tattoos you can just use a general lotion.

It's best to use a fragrance free lotion and usually do that for about a week or two. With color tattoos is best to use the ointment for the first couple days then you can switch to lotion after a week or two sometimes I cover the color tattoo with plastic for first couple days then make sure you wash it after unwrapping each day. Just leaving the plastic on for a few hours at a time is good it will help seal in the color and keep it protected.

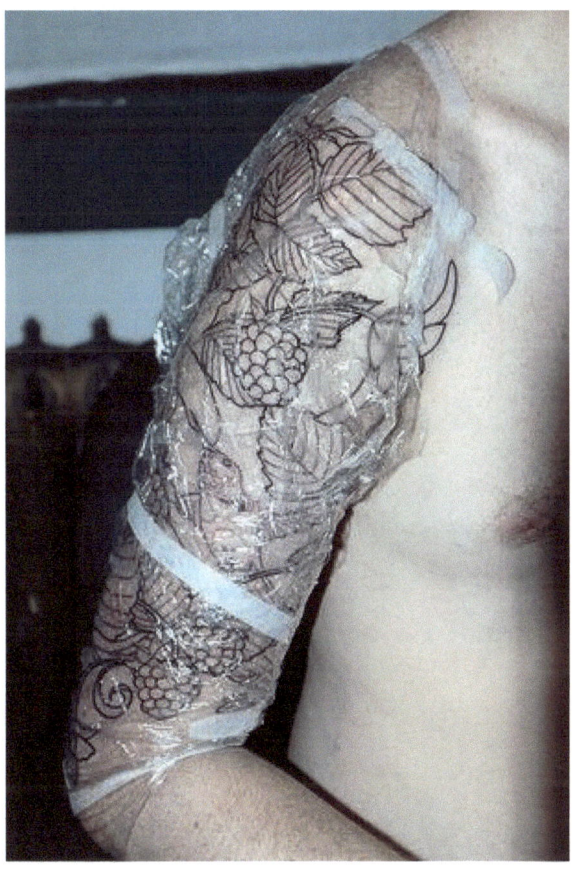

It usually can take a few weeks to a month for tattoo to fully heal dependent on how well the tattoo was done the better it will heal. My tattoos usually take about a week to two weeks for heal, about 2 weeks for just color. Some people use Aquaphor and some other things to help to heal the tattoo. As long as it has **no fragrance** is good and make sure you **don't use cocoa butter** or Vaseline.

Also be sure to not saturate the tattoo with whenever you use, just a thin coat is fine. Many people wonder if washing the tattoo the safe, **washing the tattoo is completely safe** and actually helps the healing process. The main thing is you don't want to have the tattoo on the sun the sun really hurts the tattoo it can make the tattoo sting and can negatively affect the color. It's best to use sunscreen if you're going to be out in the sun with the new tattoo but my advice is to fully cover the tattoo up if you're in the sun. Same thing with water you don't really want to get your tattoo submerged in water, especially saltwater or pool water.

Chapter 20- Apprenticeships

Now finally we are going to discuss apprenticeships, and how to get an apprenticeship.

Now I for one have apprenticed many people over the 15 years that I've been tattooing and I'll just say this if you're looking to be a tattoo apprentice, it is a lot of work. There is a lot of people trying to get into the business now, many people see how lucrative it is. Which is fine, others see an outlet for their artwork where they can actually perform their art and be paid well for it. This is totally true in tattooing.

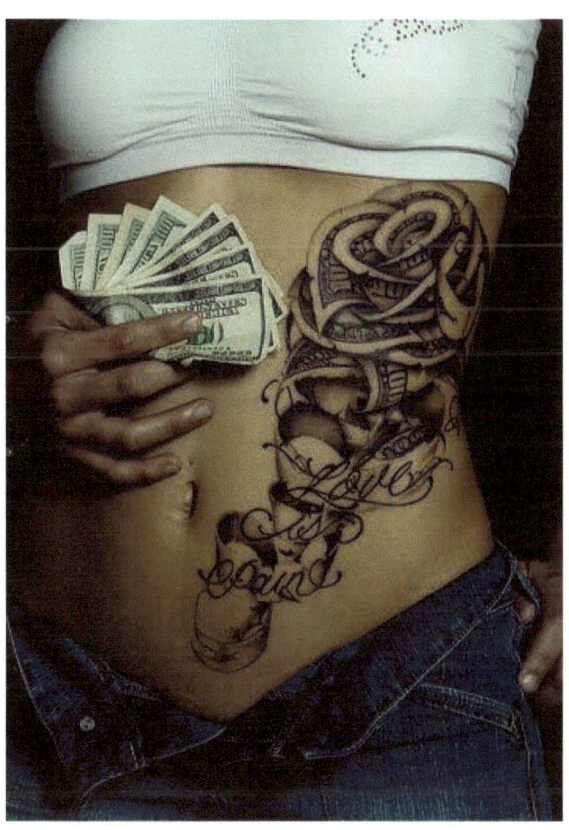

There's not always good jobs for tattoo artist to get into these days where they can make money and live a great lifestyle off of there art. Other than tattooing that is why tattooing seems like a haven for most artists. But many artists take a lax approach to getting an apprenticeship or furthering their skill tattooing. With this job you will have to be very active and able to work with customers which means customer service skills also if you want to make in this business. If you want to find a good tattoo apprenticeship you're going to need a few things in order before you start your search.

First you want to prepare a portfolio of your artwork this way you can show the tattoo shop owner that you mean business. The more impressive your artwork the better your chances are at getting an apprenticeship sometimes you may have to visit a few different shops before actually finding someone willing to give you a chance. Sometimes shops are really busy or the owner could be busy or sometimes tattoo shops are just full of artists and they might not have room for an apprentice they have to sacrifice time for.

At the same time you have to be careful when looking for shop apprenticeship, you want to learn the right way and its best to learn the right way from the start. I know many artists that were apprenticed improperly and you can still see it in their work. If you have seven years in the tattoo industry and you still can't do good line work that means there's a problem!

Presentation is also very important when trying to get an apprenticeship; tattoo shops want somebody that may represent their shop well also. You have to remember they are also taking their time to help you aswell.

On interview day you want to be properly dressed, it's obviously not a corporate office setting, but at the same time it is a business and you want to be presentable and let the boss know you're serious about the job.

Living in California have definitely seen my fair share of bad apprentices, if you walk into an interview with sunglasses on and leave them on during the interview and think you're going to get a job, good luck. But yes I have seen this happen first hand; sorry but people this ignorant simply won't make it in the tattoo industry.

Chapter 21- Local laws and licenses

Local laws and licenses

Dependent on where you live the laws are different in each state some states are more lax on the tattoo profession and some states are extremely serious on tattoo laws. I've opened up several shops in different states and one thing I always start with is Google search on the local laws online and **print out the ordinances**. This way you have a blueprint right in front of you on what it's going to take to open a shop in that county.

Even from county to county can be different so you need to know exactly what you're getting yourself into. Some states require you to even have a licensed physician on staff to get a tattoo license. I lost tons of money back once not doing my proper research on the laws first. What I do is add up everything that will be needed and that way you can put that into your expenses for when you draw up your business plan. The main cost of things that you're going to need is licensing costs which can range from $50-150 for the licensing tattoo shop, some states require each artist to be licensed thats usually around $50 per license, these will need to be renewed each year. Other expenses that you'll need that are major expenses are obviously rent and leasing fees. Build-out for your tattoo shop, all furniture and displays, the autoclave is a major investment autoclaves and can run up into the thousands of dollars.

And you also have to factor in advertising and just fixing up the shop this can cost you an additional 10k to $20,000 just for this. Advertising is extremely important if you want to get a good return on your investment. You're going to have to let people know that your shop is open for business. We will get into advertising later I have some great tips for you.

License- $150 per year

Rent - 500-1500 depending on location.

Build out- 10-20,000

Autoclave- 500-1500

Furniture- 1,000-5,000

Flash (tattoo designs)- 500-1,000

Desks- 500

Tattoo Equipment (Machines, Power supply) 500+

Advertising- 1k-20,000

So as you can see the costs can start to add up fast. What you can do is buy what you can afford and then add on as you go. There nothing wrong with that.

Chapter 22- Bookkeeping

Bookkeeping is extremely important, you want to keep track of your books from day one once you get behind it's hard to get caught up. The better you do this yourself the less you have to pay a professional. What I found that works for me over the years is an Excel file on my computer desktop in my office and I have a sheet for all artists to document their work during the day, that way I can just add it to my file each night when I count revenue from the day. Setting this up on your computer is easy and fast and utilizing it is worth its weight in gold. At the end of the year you will see.

Many people also use QuickBooks I believe it's a small payment for that and works well for many; you can also incorporate QuickBooks into your merchant account which makes it easy to keep track of money. Having a bookkeeper on staff at least part-time is good to have unless you do the books yourself that way at the end of the year it's not that much of a headache.

Also making paperwork where artists can fill out what they did that day and keeping track of all tattoos piercings done and even touchups has proven very beneficial. I try to document everything.

Chapter 23- Promotion offline

This chapter is big, so big I had to split into two parts. Listen carefully.

Local off-line promotion is the first thing to discuss, many things like the phonebook and yellow pages are outdated these days. But there are some things that really work to get your business in front of people looking for tattoo. First thing first worth mentioning is flyers, **nice flyers**, (not junk) If you really want to get good paying clients you have to show them good quality tattoo work.

Your advertising also represents your company, I cannot stress that enough. If you want to build a brand that people will come and bring you money and pay a good price for a tattoo you're going to have to conduct yourself in a professional business manner. And that extends to your advertising. Unless of course you want to do $25 scratcher tattoos all day. Which then this is not the book for you. The reason I mention flyers first is because it's been one of the fastest returns on investments I've made. **And they reach customers directly.**

You can prepare some flyers then you can easily get people from craigslist to pass out your flyers, a few thousand flyers or even a few hundred in the neighborhood can definitely work wonders for you. I've seen people come in the same day they received the flyer. Having a good flyer is also the key to if you want people to respond well to your ad.

Second worth mentioning is local newspapers, it's a little more money but these newspapers are really good, not regular newspapers nobody reads those for tattoos. I'm talking about the smaller local papers and magazines that are distributed to businesses and residences in the neighborhood the ones with the bright color ads and stuff like that. People like those and actually read them, that's where you want to be.

Try out different magazines until you find one that really gives you a good return, what I do is put a coupon in the magazine and track that coupon and see how many of those coupons that you get back into your shop. This way you will know which magazines are working best, this is crucial; many businesses don't track this or even utilize this. I have and it works great!

So try the Pennysaver's and super savers, just don't go into a commitment right away into you find out if it works or not. Many people try to sell you six months to a two-year contract do not accept that, you will be stuck paying for that advertising if it works or not. You will have to try a few magazines before you find one that works this is important or you will lose a few thousand dollars that you could've invested into advertising that does work.

Chapter 24- Promotion online

Next chapter in my favorite, online marketing.

Online marketing can be extremely lucrative for your business, these days everyone's is online or on their smartphone, so cross promoting online can definitely put you ahead of your competition. First thing first you need a website, the website doesn't have to be perfect but as long as it's not terrible it will do. As long as it's easy to navigate and update ,and you can add your pictures and information that's all you need to get started. Spending thousands on the website up front is not really needed. What is needed is branching out and expanding in your area so more customers will know about you. So the website is the first part in building your local tattoo empire.

Next, make sure you have all your social media set up like Facebook Twitter, Google +1, Yellow pages, Merchant Center, Hot frog and there's many others this is just to name a few. These are the local directories that you will want to be on; it will bring you extra traffic later.

Once you get all this setup online when people are looking for tattoos locally they will almost always run into something of yours. Rather it's your Facebook, Twitter or website. If you're just waiting for people to call it's not going to happen you have to get the word out there about your tattoo shop. Another thing to have is a member of staff to write content on your business and services which you can blog about and also share it online.

This is really powerful stuff once implemented. Preparing a press release is also great to do. Not only will people find it online. But it also gives you a powerful backlink back to your website. That way when people Google "tattoo shops" locally they will see your tattoo shop first. That's what you want! That's how you get the phone ring. Doing this regularly and you'll start to see your business grow, you'll start to see more traffic on your website and notice more phone calls. And you will also start hearing from customers how they found you on Google or somewhere online which is good to hear.

Chapter 25- Choosing a shop name

This is really important I've seen people make career suicide by picking terrible business names because at the end of the day it's a business. People that want to pay for quality tattoo don't like the thought of going into a tattoo shop named, Dead man's tattoo, Black sheep tattoo, Evil Devil tattoo, Evil blah blah blah.. I don't know how this crap began.. But I wish it would go away. And if you take a look at the shops and businesses in the tattoo industry that have been around the longest you will notice they don't have these stupid unprofessional names, think about that when you're choosing a business name.

Chapter 26- Portfolio

I discussed portfolios before but just wanted to make a quick note portfolios are extremely important in every aspect of the business your portfolio is the first thing people see and you want to make sure it's nice and clean and updated. Make sure all your pictures are clean and in focus no bleeding or bad tattoos if you have older tattoos it's best to replace those as soon as possible.

Chapter 27- In closing

I'd like to say if you're a good artist and you know how to conduct yourself and have a good mindset you can build a very lucrative career in tattooing just follow these tips and you should be fine. We also have setup a Facebook page where you can ask questions on tattooing, so if you have something that you don't feel I answered you can ask there. I hope I covered as much as I could for you. At the end of the day the best apprenticeship is done in the tattoo shop.

Hit me up on the Tattoo Facebook Page! I'll see you there:

https://www.facebook.com/TattooTrainingGuide

If you're looking for tattoo supplies, medical supplies, quality tattoo ink, or tattoo kits to get started. Please check out Dragon Tattoo Supply http://dragontattoosupplies.com

HAPPY TATTOOING!!!

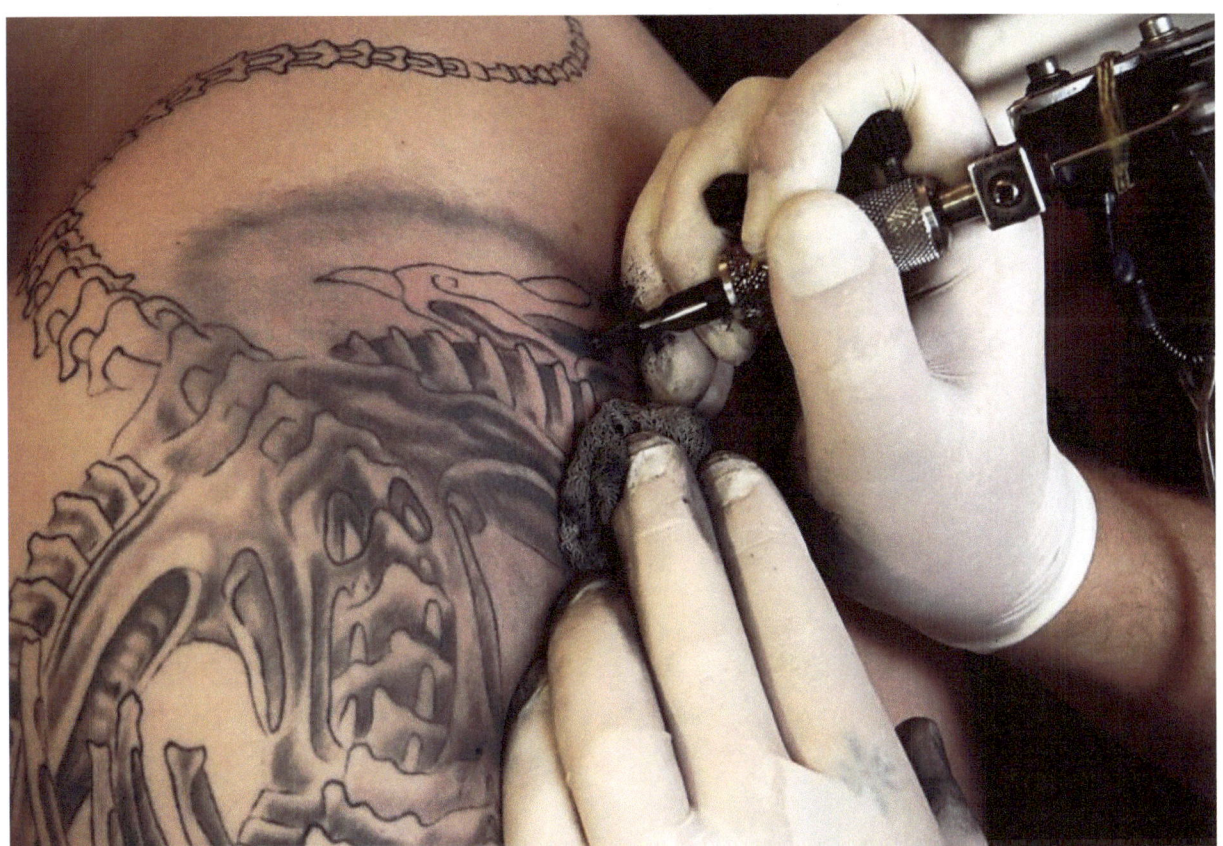

The Ultimate Tattoo Course

The Complete Tattoo Apprentice Guide

Copyright 1999-2014 by The Ultimate Tattoo Course. All Rights Reserved.

www.ingramcontent.com/pod-product-compliance
Lightning Source LLC
Chambersburg PA
CBHW040749200526
45159CB00025B/1809